MAYER SMITH

The Billionaires Love Trick

Copyright © 2025 by Mayer Smith

All rights reserved. No part of this publication may be reproduced, stored or transmitted in any form or by any means, electronic, mechanical, photocopying, recording, scanning, or otherwise without written permission from the publisher. It is illegal to copy this book, post it to a website, or distribute it by any other means without permission.

This novel is entirely a work of fiction. The names, characters and incidents portrayed in it are the work of the author's imagination. Any resemblance to actual persons, living or dead, events or localities is entirely coincidental.

Mayer Smith asserts the moral right to be identified as the author of this work.

Mayer Smith has no responsibility for the persistence or accuracy of URLs for external or third-party Internet Websites referred to in this publication and does not guarantee that any content on such Websites is, or will remain, accurate or appropriate.

Designations used by companies to distinguish their products are often claimed as trademarks. All brand names and product names used in this book and on its cover are trade names, service marks, trademarks and registered trademarks of their respective owners. The publishers and the book are not associated with any product or vendor mentioned in this book. None of the companies referenced within the book have endorsed the book.

First edition

This book was professionally typeset on Reedsy. Find out more at reedsy.com

Contents

1	The Illusion of Wealth	1
2	A Plan is Born	7
3	Starting Fresh	13
4	The Love Interest	19
5	Real Connection	24
6	The Temptation	30
7	Inner Conflict	36
8	Old Life	41
9	Confrontation	47
10	The Fallout	53
11	Reckoning	59
12	Gesture	65
13	Rebuilding Trust	71
14	New Beginning	77

One

The Illusion of Wealth

Damien Holt sat at the head of a glittering marble table, his fingers absently tracing the rim of a crystal wine glass. The banquet hall around him sparkled under the weight of opulence—golden chandeliers hanging from the ceiling, their lights casting a soft, flattering glow over the crowd below. The chatter of the high-society guests mixed with the faint, melodious strains of a string quartet playing in the corner. The finest champagne flowed, and laughter filled the air, but Damien felt a thick, almost suffocating silence inside his chest.

He glanced across the table, where his closest business partners clinked glasses in celebration. Another deal closed, another triumph. On the surface, everything looked perfect. At thirty-two, he was one of the most successful entrepreneurs in the world, the owner of a sprawling empire spanning industries from tech to luxury goods. His name was synonymous with wealth, power, and influence. He had everything—money, status, and the adoration of people who would kill to be in his position.

Yet, as he stared into the swirling depths of his glass, Damien realized that he had never felt more alone.

The people around him weren't really his friends. They weren't even his acquaintances. They were sycophants, chameleons, and opportunists who fawned over him only because of his fortune. He could see it in their eyes—the way they admired his tailored suits, his custom-made cufflinks, the watch on his wrist that could feed an entire village for a year. They didn't care about him. They cared about what he could give them.

Damien set his glass down with a soft clink. The sound was drowned out by the laughter of the guests, their faces illuminated with fake smiles, their voices bubbling with exaggerated excitement. None of them knew him—not really. He was nothing but a commodity to them, a symbol of everything they wanted to be. The thought left a bitter taste in his mouth, but it was a taste he had grown accustomed to.

He stood abruptly, his chair scraping loudly against the floor. His abrupt movement drew the attention of a few nearby guests. Their gazes followed him as he strode to the balcony, stepping out into the cool night air. The city lights below twinkled like a constellation, and the stars above seemed distant and unreachable. He rested his elbows on the stone railing, breathing in the crisp night air as he tried to clear his mind.

The Illusion of Wealth

"Everything okay, Mr. Holt?" a voice called from behind him.

He turned to see one of his assistants, a young woman named Claire, standing a few feet away. Her face was perfectly composed, though her eyes betrayed a hint of concern. She had been with him for several years now, one of the few people who had worked for him long enough to know how he operated. She, too, was a product of the system he had built—polished, professional, and always with a smile that reached just far enough to seem genuine.

"I'm fine," he said with a faint smile, turning back to the view. "Just needed some air."

Claire hesitated for a moment before stepping closer. "I've received a few calls, sir. The investors are asking about the next project. They want to know when you're going to finalize the plans for the new luxury resort in the Maldives."

Damien let out a quiet sigh. It never stopped. Even in the midst of this lavish celebration, the demands of his empire were always looming over him. The pressure never ceased, and the expectations were relentless. He wondered if he would ever have a moment where he didn't feel like the weight of the world was bearing down on him.

"Tell them I'll get back to them tomorrow," he said, his voice flat. "We'll schedule a meeting."

Claire nodded and turned to leave, but then stopped as if something had just occurred to her. "Oh, and there's someone here to see you. A reporter. They're asking for a few minutes of your time."

Damien's brow furrowed. "A reporter? What for?"

"Something about your philanthropic efforts," Claire replied. "They said it's about your latest donation to the children's hospital."

Damien rubbed the bridge of his nose. He hated interviews. He hated being put on display, being asked to speak about things that didn't matter—things that were only meant to enhance his image. The truth was, he had made the donation to avoid negative press, to quiet the critics who had started to call him out for his lack of charity. But he wasn't interested in being a philanthropist for the spotlight.

"Tell them I'm unavailable," he said curtly.

Claire hesitated but nodded. "Of course, sir."

As she walked away, Damien's thoughts drifted. The last few years had been a blur of deals, acquisitions, and endless social events. He had been everywhere, met everyone, and done everything that was expected of him. Yet, in all that time, he had never felt truly seen. No one knew him—no one ever had. And the few people who had tried to get close to him had been repelled by his detachment, his walls, his obsession with control.

He leaned against the railing, feeling the weight of his own success. It was supposed to feel fulfilling, wasn't it? He had achieved everything his younger self had dreamed of. So why did it feel like he was trapped in an endless cycle of self-imposed isolation?

His phone buzzed in his pocket, pulling him from his reverie. He pulled it out and glanced at the screen. A text message from his longtime friend and business associate, Henry:

"Another event lined up for next month. Same crowd. Same faces. You in?"

Damien stared at the message for a long time, his finger hovering over the keyboard. He knew exactly what Henry was asking: Would he show up, pretend to enjoy the company of people who only cared about his wealth, and continue playing the role of the perfect billionaire?

The truth was, Damien was tired of it. He was tired of the games, tired of the facades, tired of the endless parade of hollow connections. But he couldn't stop. He couldn't just disappear and leave it all behind. Not yet. Not until he figured out what he truly wanted.

Damien typed back a simple reply:

"Let's talk tomorrow."

He stared at the screen for a moment before locking the phone and slipping it back into his pocket. The night was still. The city was still. But inside him, a storm was brewing—a storm that had been gathering for years and was finally beginning to take shape.

What if there was more to life than this? What if the wealth, the status, the power—everything that had defined him—wasn't enough to fill the emptiness he felt? What if the life he had built was nothing more than an illusion, a gilded cage with no way out?

He turned and walked back inside the banquet hall, the sound of laughter and clinking glasses greeting him like a hollow echo. He looked around at the guests, each one a puppet dancing on strings he had pulled. They were all playing a part, just like him. All pretending. All pretending to be happy, to be content, to be fulfilled.

But Damien knew the truth. He knew that behind the smiles and the champagne, they were all just like him—trapped in a world of illusion. And as he moved through the crowd, exchanging pleasantries with faces he had known for years but never truly seen, Damien couldn't shake the feeling that he was standing on the edge of something bigger, something that would finally force him to face the one question he had been avoiding his entire life:

What would happen if he stopped pretending?

Two

A Plan is Born

The days following the gala felt like a blur to Damien Holt. The whirlwind of meetings, calls, and commitments seemed to blur together, each one more suffocating than the last. He had spent years building an empirethat sprawled across continents, commanded respect, and became a towering fortress of wealth and success. But now, it felt like a prison. Every corner he turned, every new encounter, seemed to be a reminder of just how empty his world had become.

The people who once worshiped him from afar now sought him out for their gain. Deals, investments, lucrative opportunities—they all came with strings attached. They wanted a piece of him. They wanted his approval, his influence, his money. What was left of his soul after years of sacrificing his personal life for this empire?

It wasn't the work that bothered him—he loved the thrill of business, the chase, the competition. It wasn't the wealth either, though it had become an all-consuming part of his identity. No, it was the absence of real connection, the knowledge that no one around him truly saw him for who he was. The loneliness that ate at him every night, after the parties ended and the applause faded away.

Damien sat in his office late one evening, the glow of his laptop screen casting harsh light across his face. He was staring at the stock market data, a set of numbers that barely registered in his mind. His mind was elsewhere, somewhere far beyond the financial charts and projections. He closed the laptop with a sharp click, the sudden silence of the room pressing down on him.

For the first time in years, Damien realized he wanted more than just another deal, more than another luxury hotel or multi-billion-dollar acquisition. He wanted something real. Something genuine. Something that had nothing to do with his fortune, his reputation, or his status. He wanted to be loved for who he was—just Damien. Not the billionaire, not the mogul, but the person underneath all the wealth and success.

The thought struck him like a bolt of lightning. What if he could find someone who would love him for himself, not his money? What if there was a way to remove all the trappings of his wealth and see if someone would still want him for who he really was? A plan began to take shape in his mind, one that felt almost reckless in its audacity.

A Plan is Born

Damien leaned back in his chair, rubbing his temples as he thought through the details. He couldn't keep living like this, pretending to be happy while drowning in a sea of fake relationships and superficial connections. He needed a way out. A way to reset everything, to test the waters and find out if there was someone out there who could see past the persona of "Damien Holt, billionaire."

What if he disappeared?

Not physically, but in a way that would force people to look beyond the wealth and focus on him as a person. What if he could find someone who didn't care about his financial status, someone who could see him for who he really was? The idea began to grow in his mind, and with it came a strange sense of clarity.

"I could be anyone," he muttered to himself. "I don't need all of this."

Damien's eyes fell on the sleek, polished watch on his wrist, a gift from one of his business partners. It cost more than most people made in a year. But to him, it was nothing more than a symbol—a mark of his success. But it was also a constant reminder of the thing that had isolated him from the world. Everything he had, everything he wore, every inch of his life was a mask. It wasn't real.

The plan began to form, piece by piece. It would take careful execution, and it would require him to step into a life he had never truly known—a life where he wasn't surrounded by luxury, but instead, by the ordinary, the everyday. It would mean abandoning his status, his connections, and his wealth. For a while, at least. He would need to shed every ounce of his former self and become someone else entirely.

Damien thought about it for a moment longer, considering the consequences. He could walk away from his company, disappear from the public eye, and start over. But would it be worth it? Could he really find love this way? He didn't know, but the idea of continuing down his current path, filled with hollow interactions and empty gestures, was unbearable.

He stood up abruptly, his chair scraping against the floor, and paced across the room. The decision had been made. There was no turning back. He was going to do it. He was going to walk away from everything—his wealth, his status, and most importantly, his empire—for the sake of something more meaningful. Something real.

Damien picked up his phone and made the call. He needed to speak with his most trusted assistant, Claire. She had been with him for years and was one of the few people who knew him outside of the business world. She was loyal, dependable, and the only person he trusted with his plans. He knew it would be a difficult conversation, but there was no other way.

When Claire answered, her voice was calm, as always. "Mr. Holt, how can I help you?"

"I need you to arrange something for me," Damien said, his voice steady. "I'm going to step away from the business for a

A Plan is Born

while. I need to disappear."

There was a long pause on the other end. Claire was likely processing the weight of his words. "Sir, are you sure about this?" she asked carefully. "This isn't like you. You've built this company from the ground up."

"I know," he said, cutting her off. "But I need to get away. I need to find something real."

Another pause, this one longer than the first. "I understand, sir," Claire said quietly. "But what about the company? What about your responsibilities?"

"I'll handle everything," Damien replied. "I trust you'll take care of things in my absence."

"Of course, Mr. Holt," Claire said. "I'll handle it all. But please… be careful."

Damien hung up the phone and exhaled, feeling the weight of his decision settle on his shoulders. This was just the beginning. There would be no going back once he started down this path. But he couldn't help feeling a spark of excitement, a glimmer of hope that perhaps, just perhaps, he would find the love he had been searching for all his life—free from the expectations of wealth, free from the illusions that had kept him trapped for so long.

He didn't know what awaited him, but for the first time in years, he felt a sense of possibility that was brighter than the glittering lights of his former world. The plan was set in motion, and all that remained was for him to follow it through.

Three

Starting Fresh

The first thing Damien Holt did was get rid of everything.

He walked through his penthouse that morning, staring at the sleek furniture, the art pieces from renowned international galleries, the polished wood floors that gleamed like they were constantly under the careful scrutiny of a team of servants. Everything in the apartment screamed excess, indulgence, and the life of a man who had everything.

It was all gone.

He started with the clothes. His wardrobe, a veritable shrine to wealth and influence, was stripped bare. The tailored suits, the shirts made from the finest Egyptian cotton, the hand-made Italian shoes—each piece was carefully packed and stored, and it felt almost like losing a part of himself. But he knew he had to. He couldn't pretend anymore, not even to himself. He needed a clean slate, and that meant leaving behind every last bit of his old life.

Then came the cars—the fleet of luxury vehicles that had once been a symbol of his power. Damien had always found a strange comfort in his sports cars, the roar of the engines, the way the leather seats cradled his body as he drove through the city streets. But now, they seemed like a shackle. He arranged for them to be sold. The first time the Ferrari and the Porsche were driven away from his garage, it felt like an enormous weight had been lifted off his shoulders, even as he watched their taillights disappear into the distance.

His phone was next. The sleek device, which had once buzzed non-stop with messages from investors, clients, and acquaintances, was silenced. For a moment, he stared at the screen, uncertain. It had been his lifeline for years—his connection to the world. But he was about to enter a new phase of his life, one where he wouldn't need the constant reminders of who he used to be. Damien deleted the contacts, the apps, the photos—everything. All he had left now was the raw truth of his decision.

Damien packed a single suitcase—nothing more. He filled it with simple clothes, jeans, plain shirts, shoes that didn't gleam with the telltale polish of wealth. It felt surreal, the weight of the clothing lighter, the choices simpler. He closed the suitcase and, for the first time in years, felt an unfamiliar sensation—relief.

Starting Fresh

That afternoon, he walked out of his penthouse, leaving behind the penthouse views of the city skyline. The elevator doors closed behind him, and as the building descended, he could hear the soft hum of the machinery—a sound that had always been a part of his life. But today, it felt distant, foreign. He was not Damien Holt, the billionaire mogul, anymore. He was something else. Someone else. A man ready to start fresh.

—-

He arrived at his new apartment late that evening, the building a far cry from the luxurious glass towers he was used to. It was a modest building in an older part of the city, its brick walls worn with age and the paint peeling in places. The lobby was dimly lit, and there was a smell of old wood and faint dampness in the air. But as he stood there, waiting for the elevator to take him to the third floor, Damien felt a rush of exhilaration. This was it. This was real.

The apartment, when he finally entered, was small and sparsely furnished—a worn-out couch, a coffee table that had clearly seen better days, and a small kitchenette that looked more like an afterthought. The walls were bare, save for a few photos from previous tenants that had been left behind. It was a far cry from the immaculate, designer spaces he had lived in for years. But it was all he needed.

Damien spent the first night on the couch, sleeping fitfully as his mind raced. In the morning, he forced himself to wake early. It felt strange—no staff, no assistants, no schedules to follow. It was just him. For the first time in ages, the silence wasn't oppressive—it was freeing. He didn't have to answer to anyone. No one expected anything from him. No meetings, no phone calls, no one watching his every move.

But as the days passed, the novelty of simplicity started to fade, replaced by a gnawing uncertainty. Damien hadn't truly realized just how isolated he had become until he was no longer surrounded by his empire. The life he had carefully built, the one that had defined him, had given him purpose. It had been a system—flawless, predictable, and now, it was gone. The world he had spent years mastering felt like a distant memory. He had chosen this life, yes, but now that he was here, he wasn't sure what to do with it.

The first few weeks were a blur of small steps. Damien got a job at a local café down the street. It was as menial as he could have imagined—sweeping floors, wiping down counters, serving coffee to people who barely gave him a second glance. He kept his head down, doing the work with an almost obsessive focus. It was humbling, and yet, there was a certain satisfaction in the simplicity of it. At the end of the day, no one cared who he was, and for the first time in years, no one expected anything from him. No one looked at him and saw the face of a billionaire, the owner of a sprawling tech empire. He was just another guy.

He wore plain clothes—nothing expensive or attention-grabbing. He didn't own anything that screamed money. His hands, once manicured and polished, were now calloused from the work. He had no assistant to smooth over problems or to filter out the trivialities of daily life. When the coffee machine broke down, it was Damien who had to fix it. When the cashier at the register had an issue with the register, it was Damien who stepped in to help. The work wasn't glamorous, but it gave him a sense of purpose—a small sense of control that had eluded him for so long.

—-

One afternoon, as Damien was setting up tables outside the café, a woman walked by. He had seen her around a few times, but today, she caught his attention. She had the kind of presence that made people look twice. Her dark hair fell in loose waves down her back, and she wore simple clothes—jeans and a black hoodie—but there was something about the way she carried herself that made her stand out. Her eyes were focused, determined, as though she had a destination in mind, and yet, when she passed by Damien, she glanced at him, a faint smile tugging at her lips.

He was struck, not just by her appearance but by the sense of familiarity. She wasn't like the others. There was something raw and unpretentious about her. She wasn't looking at him like everyone else had. She wasn't waiting for him to give her something, to provide her with something. She wasn't interested in his wealth. She was just… there. And for some strange reason, that made him feel both nervous and exhilarated.

The woman stopped just a few feet away from him. She looked back at the café's sign.

"This place has great reviews," she said, her voice soft but confident. "I've been meaning to try it."

Damien glanced at her, a little caught off guard by her sudden interest. "It's not bad," he said, his voice quieter than he had intended. "Best coffee in the area."

She smiled again, and Damien felt something stir within him, something unfamiliar. She wasn't waiting for him to make an introduction, to offer her something. She wasn't impressed by the café or by anything he could offer. She was simply… engaging with him. He hadn't had a conversation like this in so long. It was strange, but it was also real.

"I'll give it a shot," she said, taking a step closer. "Maybe I'll see you around."

As she walked inside, Damien stood there for a long moment, watching her retreating figure. He hadn't even realized how much he had missed the simple human connection.

In that moment, he knew one thing for certain. His plan—his fresh start—had just begun.

Four

The Love Interest

The morning air felt different. It wasn't the crisp, invigorating chill of winter, nor the sticky heat of summer. It was something in between, the kind of weather that lingered in the city like a secret waiting to be uncovered. Damien hadn't expected it to feel this way—this strange sense of anticipation. It was like stepping into a new chapter of his life, and every step he took seemed to carry a weight that wasn't entirely unpleasant. He wasn't sure where this path would lead, but for the first time in a long while, he didn't feel the need to control every outcome.

He walked down the narrow street from his new apartment, a coffee in hand, eyes scanning the world around him. The place was quieter than he expected. Small cafes, neighborhood markets, and antique shops lined the streets, their facades weathered by time, but each place seemed to pulse with a quiet life that was foreign to him. There were no glossy billboards, no flashy lights, no reminders of his past life. There was only the hum of a city that didn't know who he was, and that felt liberating.

At the corner, he paused, watching an elderly woman haggle with a vendor over the price of apples. Her laughter, rough and genuine, broke the silence of the morning, and it made Damien smile. Life here was real—raw in its simplicity. There were no facades, no expectations. And in that moment, he felt like he was exactly where he needed to be.

He continued down the street, his pace slowing as he approached a small, unassuming café nestled between a used bookstore and an art gallery. It was the kind of place that looked like it had been around forever, with mismatched furniture and a chalkboard sign out front advertising daily specials. The smell of freshly ground coffee and baked pastries spilled into the street, and without thinking, Damien pushed open the door.

The bell above the door chimed softly as he stepped inside, his senses immediately enveloped by the warmth of the space. The dim light, the soft murmur of conversations, the clink of ceramic mugs—it was all so different from the polished, sterile luxury he was accustomed to. It felt… human.

Damien took a seat at the bar, ordering a black coffee and glancing around. The café was small but cozy, with a few regulars chatting quietly at tables, and a couple of college students hunched over their laptops. The woman behind the counter was busy preparing drinks, her dark hair pulled back into a messy bun, her hands moving with a practiced ease as she worked. She wore a faded denim apron, and her eyes were focused on the task at hand, but there was an unmistakable sense of calm about her.

Damien watched her for a moment, intrigued by the way she seemed so perfectly in sync with the space. She didn't wear a designer outfit or have an air of pretension about her. She was simply… herself. And it felt like a breath of fresh air.

When she finally turned to place his coffee on the counter, her eyes met his. For a moment, he wasn't sure what he was looking at. Her gaze was sharp, intelligent, but there was something else there—something almost cautious, as if she was sizing him up in the same way he had spent years sizing up the world. She didn't smile, but she didn't look away either. She simply nodded, a silent acknowledgment that he was there.

"Anything else?" she asked, her voice low but warm.

Damien hesitated for a moment, surprised by the lack of small talk. Most people would have given him a compliment or asked about his day—something shallow, a pleasantry to keep the interaction going. But she didn't. She just… existed in the moment.

"No, this is perfect," he said, his voice sounding foreign to his own ears. It had been so long since he'd had a real conversation with anyone not driven by an agenda.

She nodded again and moved away to serve another customer.

Damien took a sip of his coffee, savoring the rich, bitter taste. It was a far cry from the fancy lattes he used to drink, the ones made with gold-leafed syrups and the finest European beans. But this—this felt real. It felt like life was happening here in the most ordinary, imperfect way.

The woman behind the counter caught his eye again as she wiped down the counter, her gaze briefly flickering over him before returning to the task at hand. There was a cool detachment in her demeanor, a sense of guardedness that piqued his curiosity. She wasn't pretending to be anything, and she wasn't interested in making him feel special. That, perhaps, was what made her stand out to him.

He watched her for a while, unsure of why he couldn't look away. She wasn't beautiful in the traditional sense—not in the way that women in his past had been, all manicured and polished with the right brand names and the right image. But there was something striking about her, a quiet strength that was reflected in the way she moved and interacted with the world around her. It was different from anything he had ever encountered.

After a few moments, she looked up, her expression unreadable, before she spoke again. "You've been staring at me for a while," she said, her tone dry but not unkind.

Damien's lips quirked slightly in surprise. No one had ever spoken to him like that before—no one had ever been so direct. Most people either fawned over him or tried to be overly deferential. But this woman was… unbothered by him. And in that unspoken challenge, something stirred in him.

"I was just thinking," he said, his voice light, though his heart beat faster than he expected. "About how unusual it is to meet someone who doesn't care about who I am."

She raised an eyebrow, her expression thoughtful. "I didn't know I was supposed to care."

Damien smiled, the edges of his tension loosening. "Most people do."

She gave him a wry smile before turning back to her work, but Damien noticed the slight flicker of interest in her eyes. He wasn't sure if she was intrigued by him or simply curious, but it was the first time in ages that he felt like someone might be seeing him—not as a billionaire, not as the business tycoon everyone thought they knew, but just as a person.

He wanted to know more about her. He wanted to hear her story, understand the layers beneath her calm exterior. But something told him that wasn't going to happen easily. She was not the kind of woman who gave herself away. She was a puzzle—one that Damien couldn't wait to try and solve.

As he finished his coffee, he couldn't shake the feeling that this encounter—this woman—was going to change everything.

Five

Real Connection

Damien couldn't stop thinking about her.

The days after their first encounter at the café felt like a blur. Each morning, he found himself gravitating toward that same little spot on the corner of the street, the one with the unassuming café and the quiet woman behind the counter. Her name, he had learned, was Elena, a simple, unpretentious name that seemed to match her personality. She hadn't been like anyone else he had ever met. The kind of woman who didn't care about his money, who didn't seem to recognize him as the billionaire mogul. She was just there—present, unbothered by the weight of expectations that seemed to crush everyone else around him.

Each day, Damien returned to the café. The small interactions, the casual greetings, the fleeting moments of eye contact—

they were enough to keep him coming back. Elena didn't ask questions. She didn't pry into his life. And in a world where everyone seemed to want something from him, that felt like a gift.

It was late in the afternoon, just after the lunch rush had died down, when the real change began. Damien had just finished his usual black coffee and was about to leave when Elena caught his eye. She was wiping down the counter, but her movements slowed as her gaze settled on him.

"You're not in a hurry today," she said, her voice casual, as if she were simply making an observation.

Damien paused, surprised by the comment. He had never given any indication that he was always rushing, but she noticed. Elena noticed.

"I suppose not," he said, his voice betraying a hint of amusement.

"You usually leave quickly," she added, continuing her work. "I figured you had somewhere important to be."

Damien took a step closer to the counter, his heart beating a little faster than usual. There was something about her—something unspoken between them that seemed to pull him in.

"I guess you could say I'm important, but not in the way most people think," he said, his words deliberate, as if testing the waters.

Elena raised an eyebrow but didn't reply right away. Instead, she continued wiping the counter, seemingly lost in thought. Damien's eyes followed her every movement, the way she methodically cleaned, the ease in her motions. She was no longer just the woman behind the counter; she was a puzzle, one that he couldn't quite figure out.

"I don't think I've seen you around before," Elena said, finally breaking the silence. Her eyes met his again, this time with an intensity that felt almost calculated, as if she was trying to read him. "You must be new to the area."

"I've been here a few weeks," he replied, his voice quieter now, careful. "Just... adjusting to life, I guess."

"Adjusting to life," Elena repeated, nodding thoughtfully. "That sounds vague."

Damien smiled, despite himself. "It is. But I suppose it's fitting."

There was something about the way she spoke that intrigued him—her ability to pick apart his words, to recognize when he was holding something back, when he was hiding. It was as if she could sense the layers beneath his carefully constructed facade.

"So, adjusting to life... what does that look like for you?" Elena asked, her voice soft, but sharp with curiosity.

Damien paused, unsure of how to answer. He had been used to talking about business, about his successes, about acquisitions and developments. But none of that seemed relevant here. None of it seemed to matter. Not to her. She wasn't asking about his wealth or his empire. She wasn't asking about his past. She just wanted to know about him. The real him, not the version the world knew.

"I guess it looks like this," he said, gesturing around the small café. "Sitting at a counter, having coffee with a stranger."

Elena didn't respond right away. She simply stood there, leaning against the counter, her expression unreadable. The silence stretched between them, heavy and pregnant with something neither of them wanted to acknowledge.

"So, what do you do when you're not adjusting to life?" she asked, her voice breaking the quiet.

Damien leaned in slightly, intrigued by her question. "I'm... figuring that out."

Elena chuckled softly, the sound low and genuine. "I hope you find something that fits."

He wanted to tell her more. He wanted to explain why he had come to this place, why he had left everything behind. But he didn't. Instead, he simply nodded, his thoughts swirling.

"You seem like someone who likes to figure things out," Elena added, her gaze piercing. "But that's the thing about life. You can't always figure it out. Sometimes, you have to live it, just... live it."

Damien swallowed, his throat suddenly dry. She was right. He couldn't always control everything. He couldn't always plan the future, make the next big move, acquire the next company. Some things had to be left to chance, to spontaneity.

He laughed, the sound low and uncertain. "I'm not used to living like that."

Elena smiled slightly, a flicker of something in her eyes. "I think that's the problem."

The air between them felt charged now, the words they exchanged more than just pleasantries. There was something unspoken, a connection forming, subtle but undeniable. Damien found himself wanting to stay, to hear more, to understand her in a way that had nothing to do with wealth or status. She was real, and in a world where everything felt manufactured, that was the most refreshing thing he had encountered in years.

"How long have you been doing this?" he asked, his curiosity getting the better of him.

Elena paused, as though surprised by the question. "A few years. I've always loved coffee," she said with a shrug, her eyes flickering to the machine behind her. "But it's not just about the coffee. It's about the people. This place… it's a little piece of everything. You know?"

Damien nodded slowly, a strange sense of calm settling over him. This was new. This was different. He wasn't just talking to someone to pass the time. He was actually connecting.

"I think I'd like that," he said quietly.

Elena's eyes softened, though she quickly masked it with her usual stoic demeanor. "It's not for everyone," she replied. "But… I think you'll figure it out."

Damien wanted to stay longer. He wanted to ask her about her life, her dreams, her thoughts on the world, but the moment was fragile, like a delicate thread that might snap if pulled too tight. And so, he stood there for a long moment, simply looking at her, until he realized he had overstayed his welcome.

"I should go," he said finally, his voice hushed.

Elena nodded, her gaze holding his for a second longer than usual. "I'll see you tomorrow."

The words hung in the air between them, almost a promise, a shared understanding that things were shifting. Damien left the café with his heart pounding, his mind racing. For the first time in years, he felt something he hadn't been prepared for—hope.

Six

The Temptation

The sun hung low in the sky, casting a warm amber glow over the city. The streets outside the café were bathed in the late afternoon light, the familiar sounds of the city hum blending with the soft rustling of leaves in the breeze. For most people, it was just another ordinary day, but for Damien, it felt like the weight of the world had settled on his shoulders.

He sat at his usual spot by the window, a cappuccino in front of him, barely touched. His fingers traced the rim of the mug, his mind far away. He had been coming to this café for weeks now, building a routine that felt both foreign and comforting. But this routine had brought with it something he hadn't anticipated: Elena.

She had become more than just the woman who served his

coffee every morning. She had become a constant, a small but significant part of his life. And the strange thing was, he wasn't sure if she even noticed. She never asked about him beyond the surface level. She didn't push him to reveal anything about his life. She just… accepted him. And that made it all the more difficult to ignore the growing pull he felt toward her.

Every day, their conversations grew a little deeper. At first, they were simple exchanges—brief comments on the weather, casual musings about the books they were reading. But little by little, those exchanges had turned into something more. They had begun to share bits of their lives, fragments of themselves that no one else seemed to care about. Elena, with her quiet confidence, had become the person Damien found himself drawn to in ways he hadn't expected.

It wasn't just the absence of expectation that fascinated him. It was the way she saw the world—without the filter of wealth, ambition, or status. She was real. Raw, even. She spoke with a kind of honesty that Damien wasn't used to. And he found himself wanting to give her the same in return.

But there was a problem.

He was lying.

Damien had been lying from the very beginning, and every day that passed, the weight of that lie grew heavier. He hadn't told her who he really was. He hadn't told her that the coffee shop he frequented wasn't his only world, that the life he had left behind was one of unimaginable wealth and power. He hadn't told her that he was Damien Holt, the man who could buy anything he wanted and destroy anyone who stood in his way.

And with every moment he spent with her, every conversation that moved a little closer to real, he felt the temptation to tell her, to come clean. He wanted to tell her everything—to rip down the walls he had built around himself and reveal the truth. But fear held him back. Fear of losing the one person in his life who didn't want something from him. Fear of losing the only genuine connection he had in years.

Damien's gaze flickered to Elena, who was now clearing a table near the window, her movements graceful, almost effortless. She seemed completely at ease in this place, in this life. And there, in the quiet solitude of the café, he wondered: what would happen if she knew the truth? What would happen if she found out who he really was?

He thought about it for a moment—imagined the look on her face when he told her. Would she be angry? Disappointed? Would she feel betrayed? Or would she, like so many others, see him for what he was—just another rich man playing games with people's emotions?

His thoughts were interrupted by the sound of Elena's voice. She was standing in front of him now, her face alight with curiosity.

"Did you finish your book?" she asked, referring to the novel he had been reading over the past few days. It was a thick, historical drama, one that had become his escape from the suffocating world he had built.

Damien looked up at her, startled for a moment. She had been asking about his book for a few days now, each time with genuine interest. And each time, he had told her just enough to keep the conversation going, to avoid revealing anything deeper about himself. It was all surface-level. Safe.

But today, it didn't feel safe. Today, the temptation to tell her the truth was almost overwhelming.

"Not yet," he said, his voice rougher than he intended. "It's been hard to find the time."

Elena raised an eyebrow, her lips curving into a small smile. "I figured. You always seem to be in a rush."

Damien shifted uncomfortably in his seat. She was right, of course. He had always been in a rush. It had been his way of life for so long. The constant push, the relentless pace, the need to stay ahead of everyone else—it had been his driving force. But now, sitting in front of her, all that seemed meaningless. What was the point of all that if he couldn't even be honest with the one person who seemed to see through the façade?

"Yeah," he said softly. "I suppose I am."

There was a moment of silence between them, a stillness that seemed to hang in the air. Elena looked at him, really looked at him, as if she were trying to understand the words he hadn't spoken. And for the first time since meeting her, Damien felt a pang of something—guilt, perhaps. Or maybe regret.

"You know," Elena said after a long pause, her voice gentle but firm, "you don't have to rush here. I mean, if you really want to finish that book, you could just take your time, come back whenever. No one's forcing you to be in a hurry."

Her words, simple and sincere, cut through him like a knife. No one had ever said anything like that to him before. No one had ever told him to slow down, to stop and live rather than constantly push forward.

Damien closed his eyes for a brief moment, the weight of her words pressing down on him. His hand tightened around the handle of his coffee cup, his fingers trembling slightly. It was too much. The guilt, the temptation, the desire to tell her everything—it was all rushing at him at once.

Tell her, a voice inside him whispered. Tell her who you really are. Let her see you for who you are, not the person you've pretended to be.

But as the words formed in his mind, another part of him recoiled. What if she rejects you? What if she sees you as nothing but a rich man with a messed-up sense of what love is?

He felt his heart beat faster, the conflict inside him growing stronger. Should he open up to her, risk it all? Or should he continue with the lie, knowing that every moment he spent with her was only building a wall between them—one that would eventually come crashing down?

His mind was spinning, and before he could say anything, Elena smiled softly, as if sensing his inner turmoil.

"You okay?" she asked quietly. "You seem... lost."

Damien hesitated, his mouth dry. He wanted to say something, anything, but the words stuck in his throat.

"I'm fine," he said finally, forcing a smile. It was a lie. He was far from fine.

But it was all he could manage.

Elena nodded, accepting his answer without question. But Damien couldn't help but feel that the moment, the chance to tell her the truth, was slipping away. And with it, the one real connection he had ever felt in his life.

Seven

Inner Conflict

T he café was quieter than usual. The hum of conversations had tapered off, the clink of coffee cups was softer, and even the buzz of the espresso machine seemed to blend into the background. Outside, the world was changing—nightfall was creeping across the city, casting shadows that seemed to stretch long and threatening, as if echoing the dark thoughts Damien had been battling inside for weeks.

He sat alone at his usual spot, his coffee cold and untouched, his gaze fixed on the half-empty mug. His mind had become a battlefield—a warzone between the man he had been and the man he wanted to become. The life he had left behind, with all its wealth, power, and empty interactions, was gnawing at the edges of his consciousness, demanding his attention. But the life he was building, the life that involved quiet mornings in this humble café and fleeting conversations with Elena, was like a soft whisper that refused to let go.

Damien had never been good at handling inner turmoil. In business, in life, he had always been a man of action. He made decisions swiftly, calculated every move with precision. But this—this was different. The longer he stayed in this small, quiet corner of the world, the more the temptation to tell Elena the truth gnawed at him. The pressure was mounting, the fear was growing, and yet, there was something even more terrifying than facing her reaction.

It was the fear of losing her.

He thought of the life he had been leading, of the hollow relationships that only existed because of his wealth. He thought of the endless streams of people who had come and gone, all seeking something from him. People who had used him, admired him, feared him, but never loved him. Never really cared for him. And then there was Elena—someone who didn't want anything from him. Someone who had made it clear from the beginning that she saw past the surface. Someone who, in her own way, seemed to understand him without the need for pretense.

But how long could he keep up the charade? How long could he live a lie and pretend that nothing was wrong? Every time she asked him something, every time she smiled at him, every time their conversations veered just a little too close to personal, it felt like a thread was being pulled. It was only a matter of time before it unraveled completely. And when it did—what would be left?

Damien stood abruptly, his chair scraping against the floor as he turned to leave. He needed air. He needed to think. The walls of the café, which had once felt like a sanctuary, were now closing in on him, suffocating him with the weight of his own thoughts. The world outside was still bathed in the soft, orange glow of the setting sun. The streets were quieter, more reflective now. The city had slowed, and so had his heart.

He walked aimlessly for a while, his feet taking him through narrow alleys, along streets that had seen better days. The city was alive, full of stories, full of lives being lived. But Damien felt like an outsider. He wasn't part of it. Not anymore.

His mind kept drifting back to Elena. To her laugh, the way she always tilted her head when she asked a question, the way her eyes would light up when she talked about her favorite books, or a movie she had seen. She was vibrant in a way that he hadn't seen in a long time. She was real. And that was what terrified him. Real people didn't belong in his world. People like Elena didn't fit into the polished, artificial life he had created.

But the longer he was around her, the more he realized he didn't want to go back to that world. He didn't want to be the man who bought his way through life, the man who had to keep people at arm's length, the man who traded authenticity for comfort and security. He didn't want to hide anymore.

Damien stopped at a park bench, the cool metal against his palms grounding him. He took a deep breath and stared out at the dusky sky. The stars had begun to peek through, small glimmers of light in a sea of dark. For a moment, he wondered if they could see him. If they could see the man he used to be. He wondered if they would judge him the way he judged himself.

The temptation to tell Elena the truth was overwhelming. But the fear of losing her—the fear of seeing that spark of interest and curiosity in her eyes disappear, replaced with disappointment, or worse, pity—was a demon he couldn't shake.

And yet, every day he kept the truth from her, every day he danced around his past, the guilt ate at him more. He was used to being decisive, to being in control, but this was something else entirely. It was the kind of decision that could change everything. A decision that could cost him the one real connection he had ever made, or… a decision that could finally set him free.

His phone buzzed in his pocket, snapping him out of his spiraling thoughts. It was a text from Claire, one of his few remaining business associates. The message was short: We need to talk. Urgent. Can you meet tomorrow?

Damien felt a surge of frustration. He had left his world behind—why was it still chasing him? He wasn't supposed to be the man who took meetings or dealt with investments anymore. He wasn't supposed to care about the numbers, the deals, the deals that he could close with a single signature. He was done with that life. Or so he thought.

He pocketed the phone and exhaled sharply. As the night deepened, the city seemed to press closer. Every corner held a shadow of something he wanted to forget, every streetlamp a reminder of the darkness he had left behind. But Elena was different. She wasn't like anyone else he had known. She hadn't asked for anything from him. She hadn't asked for his money or his time or his attention. She had simply been… there. In the most unexpected way, she had given him something he hadn't even known he needed—a glimpse of a life beyond the one he had built.

He stood up from the bench, his decision made. He wasn't going to run anymore. He wasn't going to hide behind the wall of wealth and status. If he wanted to find out what life with Elena could be, if he wanted to know what it felt like to be truly seen, then he would have to tear down the walls.

It was time to tell her the truth.

And the thought, oddly enough, filled him with something he hadn't felt in a long time—hope.

Eight

Old Life

Damien didn't expect it to hit him so suddenly.

It had been weeks since he had moved into the cramped apartment on the edge of the city, weeks since he'd left behind the towering glass buildings, the never-ending meetings, the parties where everyone pretended to be friends. Weeks since he'd stopped pretending to be something he wasn't. He had finally gotten used to the quiet, the simplicity of his new routine, the gentle rhythm of life at the café. And yet, as he walked down the street, a familiar sound broke through the peace—one that felt jarring and intrusive in this new life he was trying to build.

A sleek black car idled at the curb, the engine purring like a predator, waiting. The back window lowered, revealing the face he had been trying so hard to forget.

"Damien."

The voice came from the driver's side, smooth and authoritative, like a command. The car was too polished, too perfect, too familiar. It was as though the world he had worked so hard to escape had come rushing back in a single instant.

Damien stopped in his tracks, his breath catching in his chest. For a moment, he stood frozen, staring at the car, the temptation of the old life beckoning him like a dark, swirling vortex. He hadn't heard from any of his old associates since he left. Not a single call, not a single email. He had disappeared from the world he had once ruled, and for that, he had been both relieved and terrified.

But now, here it was, like a ghost rising from the past, offering him the familiar comforts he had thought he'd abandoned.

"Get in, Damien. We need to talk," the voice called again, and this time, it was unmistakable.

It was Victor—the head of his former operations, the man who had managed every detail of Damien's life, from the business deals to the high-stakes negotiations, to the other side of his world, the world that Damien had tried to sever ties with.

Damien's heart raced, his mind in a whirlwind of conflicting emotions. The cold steel of the car beckoned him with a siren song, promising power, success, and the wealth he had once taken for granted. It whispered of a life where nothing was out of reach, where he was always in control, always at the center.

The world he had built had been intoxicating, seductive in a way that nothing in this new life could match.

But as he took a hesitant step forward, another thought clawed at him—Elena.

Her face flashed in his mind, her soft smile, the way her eyes never judged him. She was everything this world wasn't. She was real. Her life was grounded in something pure, something untainted by the corrupting forces that had ruled his past. He could almost hear her voice now, asking him what he was doing, questioning whether he really wanted to go back.

"Damien?" Victor's voice was closer now, and Damien realized he had been standing motionless, caught in his internal battle.

He swallowed hard, his throat dry, and with a deep breath, he took a slow step toward the car.

Victor smiled, a smile that was more a calculated gesture than a genuine expression of warmth. "Glad to see you're not completely lost, Holt," he said, his tone dripping with that same patronizing familiarity that Damien had once tolerated without a second thought. "We've been trying to reach you for weeks. You've been avoiding us."

Damien didn't respond, his jaw tightening as he slid into the plush leather seat. The interior of the car was immaculate, the air-conditioned coolness almost a comfort compared to the heat of the summer outside. As the car began to move, the city slipped by, the streets he had come to know and love slowly fading into the background.

Victor's voice broke the silence again, low and measured. "We've got business to discuss. The company's been struggling since you left. You know better than anyone that the market won't wait for anyone. There's been a shift, Damien. A massive shift. And we need you back."

Damien's fingers drummed against the armrest, his mind swirling. The company. The one thing that had always been his anchor. The one thing he had left behind without a second thought. He hadn't even realized how much he had missed it until now, the old adrenaline rush of a deal on the table, the challenge of outsmarting competitors, the thrill of being the one everyone feared and respected.

But then his thoughts drifted back to Elena. To the quiet mornings, the genuine connection they had started to build. He had built a wall around himself for so long, hiding behind the illusion of power and status, but Elena had seen past all of that. She had made him feel… human. She made him feel like someone worth caring about, not just because of what he could give, but for who he truly was.

"Damien." Victor's voice broke into his thoughts again, sharper this time. "You owe us. You know that. You can't just walk away from all this."

Damien looked out the window, his eyes narrowing as the car passed the familiar, gleaming glass buildings—the towers that had been his empire. His empire. The word felt alien now. How

Old Life

had he allowed himself to get caught up in this world again?

"I've moved on, Victor," Damien said, his voice quieter than he had intended. "I'm done with all of this. I've got a new life now."

Victor laughed, a low, dangerous sound that sent a chill down Damien's spine. "You think you can just walk away from everything? You think you can erase who you are? Who you were?"

Damien didn't respond. His mind was racing now, the old life pulling at him with invisible tendrils. He could see it all again: the boardrooms, the high-stakes meetings, the endless strings of zeros on financial reports. He could see the power he wielded, the respect that others had for him, the fear he instilled. He could see himself at the top, the world at his feet.

But then Elena's face flashed in his mind again, and the image of the café, with its worn tables and mismatched chairs, anchored him. She had given him something he hadn't known he needed—a taste of something real. She had opened his eyes to the possibility that there was more to life than money, more than the fleeting satisfaction of power.

"Victor," he said, his voice steady now, "I'm not going back."

There was a moment of stunned silence in the car. Victor's eyes, which had been sharp and commanding, narrowed in disbelief. "You can't be serious," he said, his voice laced with a dangerous edge. "Damien, this isn't just about you. This is about everything. About the company, about the legacy. You can't throw that away."

Damien leaned back in his seat, his gaze fixed on the city outside. The decision was made. It had been made the moment he had walked away from that world, the moment he had tasted what it meant to live without the chains of his past. The temptation was still there, pulling at him, but he couldn't go back. Not now. Not after everything he had learned, not after everything he had felt with Elena.

"I don't need it anymore," Damien said, his voice firm, resolute. "I don't need any of it."

Victor's face hardened, his lips curling into a thin smile. "You'll regret this, Damien," he said coldly. "You always do."

The car came to a stop, and without another word, Victor opened the door and stepped out. Damien sat there for a moment, staring at the door, at the world he had just rejected. His pulse was still racing, but this time, it wasn't from fear. It was from relief.

He had made his choice.

As the car drove away, Damien stepped out onto the sidewalk, the cool air filling his lungs. The world was still here, the same as it had been. But Damien felt lighter, freer than he had in years. He had glimpsed the old life, felt the temptation of returning to it, but in the end, he had chosen something better. Something real. And for the first time in a long time, he was sure he had made the right decision.

Nine

Confrontation

The car rolled smoothly through the streets, the hum of the engine a constant drone in the background. The city outside seemed distant, as if it were a world Damien had momentarily left behind. It wasn't the same city he had once known, the one where every street corner, every skyscraper, had been a monument to his success. This city felt different now, quieter, more intimate. It felt like a place he had come to understand in a way he never had before.

But as the car turned onto a familiar street—the one that led to his old office building—Damien felt a shiver run down his spine. His past was closing in, and there was no escaping it now. The sleek black vehicle, with its tinted windows and quiet menace, was the last remnant of the empire he had abandoned. It was the reminder of everything he had once been, everything he had worked so tirelessly to build.

Victor sat across from him, his eyes sharp and calculating, his suit a perfect reflection of the polished, controlled world that Damien had once thrived in. There was no warmth in his gaze, no hint of familiarity, just the cold calculation of a man used to getting what he wanted. Damien could feel it, the weight of Victor's expectations, like a pressure that hung heavy in the air.

"So," Victor said, breaking the silence, "you've been hiding, huh? Thought you could run away from all this. Thought you could just disappear into the shadows." His voice was smooth, almost mocking, but there was an edge beneath it, a subtle threat that Damien couldn't ignore.

"I'm not hiding," Damien replied, his voice flat, his gaze fixed on the city outside the window. "I'm just living my life."

Victor chuckled softly, leaning back in his seat. "Living your life? In a shabby little apartment, drinking overpriced coffee at a dive café? You think this is life, Damien? You think this is what you were meant for?"

Damien didn't respond immediately. His fingers tightened around the armrest, the anger bubbling just beneath the surface. The life he had built here was real—it was messy, imperfect, but it was his. It was the first time in a long time that he had felt like he was in control of his own fate.

But Victor's words stung. The weight of the old world, the one filled with power and prestige, was still there, pressing against his chest. And no matter how hard he tried to push it away, it lingered. It had always been there, lurking in the background,

Confrontation

waiting for him to slip up, to go back.

Victor's eyes gleamed with satisfaction as he watched Damien wrestle with his thoughts. He could feel the pull of the old life, too. It was in the way Damien tensed, the way his hands fidgeted, the way his gaze flickered to the city outside, as though he were trying to decide whether to stay or to return to the world that had once defined him.

"You can't outrun your past, Damien," Victor continued, his voice low and persuasive. "You think you can just walk away from everything you've built? You think you can just… disappear? That's not how this works. You're too good at what you do. Too damn good to just fade into the background."

Damien turned to face him then, his eyes locking onto Victor's with a cold intensity that sent a ripple of unease through the other man. "I'm not the man you think I am anymore," Damien said, his voice steady but laced with a quiet fury. "I don't want to be that person anymore."

Victor's smile faltered, just for a moment, before it returned, wider this time, as though he were humoring Damien's naïveté. "Oh, I see," he said slowly, almost patronizingly. "You've had an epiphany, huh? Found religion, found some peace of mind? Is that it? You think you can just walk away from the game like it never mattered?"

Damien's eyes narrowed. "I'm not walking away from anything. I'm choosing a different path. A real one."

Victor laughed, a short, humorless sound that grated against Damien's ears. "A real one?" he repeated, his voice dripping with disbelief. "You're living in a fucking rat hole, Damien. You're pretending you've found something real when all you've done is escape. You've run from everything that made you who you are."

Damien clenched his jaw. "That's where you're wrong," he said, his voice low but tinged with conviction. "I've been living a lie for so long I didn't know what the truth even looked like. But now I do. And I'm not going back."

For a moment, the car was silent, the tension between them thick and suffocating. Victor didn't speak, but Damien could feel the man's anger rising, bubbling just beneath the surface. He could see it in the way his jaw tightened, the way his hands gripped the armrests of the seat.

Finally, Victor broke the silence, his voice low and dangerous. "You think you can just walk away from all of this? From us? From me?"

Damien's eyes hardened. "You can't control me anymore, Victor. And you're damn right I'm walking away."

Victor's face twisted with fury. "You think I'm just going to let you go? After everything you've done for me, for this operation? You think you can just quit? It doesn't work that way, Damien."

A chill ran down Damien's spine. He knew what was coming next. He had seen it before—when people like Victor felt their

Confrontation

control slipping away, they didn't just let it go. They would do whatever it took to pull you back in. He had seen the way Victor operated, the ruthlessness that had made him such an effective leader.

"I'm not going back to that world," Damien said, his voice calm but filled with finality. "I'm done with it."

Victor's eyes flared with rage, and for a moment, it felt like the car itself had become a pressure cooker, the air thick with unspoken threats and violence. Victor leaned forward, his voice dropping to a dangerous whisper. "You don't get to decide that, Damien. Not after everything. You don't just walk away from me. You're mine. You always will be."

Damien's heart raced, his pulse quickening, but he held his ground. "Not anymore. I'm free, Victor. And nothing you can say or do is going to change that."

For a long moment, the two men stared at each other, the weight of their history hanging heavily between them. Then, without another word, Damien opened the door and stepped out of the car. The cold night air hit him like a wave, but he didn't flinch.

As he closed the door behind him, he caught one last glimpse of Victor's face, twisted in anger, before the car sped off into the night.

Damien stood there for a moment, his breath coming in ragged gasps, his body trembling with the adrenaline of the confrontation. He had made his choice. There was no going back.

But as he walked away, his mind couldn't shake the feeling that this was only the beginning—that the war he had just started was far from over.

Ten

The Fallout

The confrontation had been brief, but its consequences lingered like a storm cloud. Damien felt the weight of the words they had exchanged, the cold finality of Victor's parting shot still ringing in his ears. He could hear the soft click of the car door closing, the way Victor had turned without a backward glance, his tailored suit cutting through the night like a shadow. It was over now. Whatever bridge had remained between Damien and his former life was gone, burned to the ground.

He stood in the middle of the city street, the sharp chill of the evening air biting at his skin, but it wasn't the cold that had him shivering. It was the dread, the gnawing uncertainty about what was to come.

The truth was, Damien hadn't expected Victor to give up so

easily. He had known the man long enough to understand that the very idea of losing control, of watching someone slip away from the world he had built, was something that Victor would never tolerate. That confrontation was only the beginning.

Damien's pulse quickened as he made his way back to his apartment. The familiar streets, once comforting, now felt alien, as if the very ground he walked on had changed beneath him. His mind raced with the possibilities of what could come next—the threats, the intimidation, the inevitable consequences of crossing the line with people who didn't know how to take "no" for an answer.

He entered his apartment and slammed the door behind him, the sound echoing in the silence. The faint hum of the refrigerator, the creak of the floorboards beneath his feet—it all felt too quiet now, too small, as if the walls were closing in on him. He wasn't just running away from his past anymore. He had defied it, challenged it in ways that were never supposed to happen.

Damien's phone buzzed on the coffee table, the screen lighting up with a name that made his heart skip a beat: Elena.

His thumb hovered over the screen for a moment before he swiped it open.

"Hey, Damien. You didn't come by today. Is everything okay?"

The message was simple, a small gesture of concern from a woman who, somehow, had begun to mean more to him than

The Fallout

he was prepared to admit.

He stared at the message for a long moment, his mind still reeling from the confrontation, from the realization that there was no going back. The weight of his secret felt heavier than ever. If Elena knew who he truly was, what he had done, what he was capable of—would she still see him as the man he had become, or would she turn away in disgust? The very thought of losing her, of destroying the one genuine connection he had, made his stomach turn.

What was the price of honesty?

Damien paced across the room, his fingers running through his hair. The world outside had taken on a muted tone, the city lights casting long shadows through his apartment window. It felt as though the entire universe had narrowed down to a single, unspoken truth: the fallout had begun, and there was no escaping it.

He typed a quick response to Elena, his fingers trembling just slightly as he wrote: I'm fine. Just needed some time to think. I'll see you tomorrow.

It was a lie, but it was the only lie he could afford to tell. He didn't know what would happen in the next few hours, let alone the next few days. The shadows of his old life were closing in, and he wasn't sure if he could outrun them.

The phone buzzed again. Another message. This time, it was from a number he didn't recognize. The name on the screen made his blood run cold: Holt Industries.

His hand shot out to grab the phone, and he stared at the message for a long time before reading it.

"You've made your choice, Damien. But remember, the choices we make always come with consequences. We'll be watching."

The message sent a chill through him. It was a warning, clear and concise. His former life, his empire, wasn't going to let him go that easily. Victor's threats hadn't been idle. They were the beginning of something far more dangerous, far more insidious. They were the beginning of a war.

Damien sank into the couch, his head in his hands. He felt trapped, cornered by the very people he had once controlled. They had power, resources, and a network that extended far beyond what he could have ever imagined. They had the means to destroy him—his reputation, his safety, everything he had worked so hard to build.

But in the silence of the room, a thought pierced through the chaos: I won't go back.

It was a simple statement, but it held weight. He wasn't going to let them drag him back into the life he had fought so hard to leave. He had made his choice, and there was no turning back. No matter the cost.

His phone buzzed again, and this time, it was a call. The number was unfamiliar, but the voice on the other end was unmistakable.

"Damien," Victor's voice came through, smooth and unbothered, as if nothing had happened between them. "We're going to have to handle this differently. You've made your decision, but that doesn't mean you won't be held accountable."

Damien's grip tightened on the phone. "What do you want from me, Victor?" he asked, his voice low, steady. "You've made your point."

Victor's laugh echoed in his ear, cold and humorless. "It's not about what I want from you, Damien. It's about what you'll lose if you don't play along. You think you can run away? You think you can just walk away from everything you've built? You can't. Not without consequences."

The line went silent for a moment, and Damien could almost hear Victor's smile.

"You'll be hearing from us soon," Victor continued, his tone now laced with a dark finality. "And this time, you won't have a choice."

The call ended abruptly, and Damien sat in the silence that followed. The weight of the threat hung in the air, thick and suffocating.

He was no longer just trying to escape the past—he was fighting it. And there was no telling how far they would go to make sure he paid for his defiance.

The door to his apartment creaked open, and Damien froze. He hadn't heard anyone enter, but there she was, standing in the doorway. Elena.

She looked at him with concern in her eyes, her brow furrowed, her arms crossed protectively over her chest. "Damien, what's going on?" she asked softly, stepping inside.

Damien opened his mouth to speak, but the words died in his throat. The truth was there, just beyond his reach, but it felt like a chasm too wide to cross. If he told her, everything would change. She would know.

But as he looked at her, standing there, so calm, so real, a decision settled in his chest.

The storm was coming. And he wasn't sure if it would destroy him or set him free.

Eleven

Reckoning

The ringing of the phone was the only sound in the apartment, loud and insistent, like a warning. Damien's hand trembled as he picked up the receiver, his heart pounding in his chest. For a moment, he simply stared at the screen, the words "Holt Industries" glaring back at him in cold, black letters. His pulse thudded in his ears, drowning out everything else.

The name, the corporation he had once led with a grip of iron, seemed like a ghost, a specter from a life that should have been left behind. He had thought he was free—free of the empire, the deals, the weight of his own legacy. He had thought that stepping away from it all, hiding out in his small apartment, away from the glittering towers and endless power struggles, would give him peace.

But the call proved otherwise.

Damien closed his eyes briefly, trying to steady himself. He wasn't going to let the past dictate his present. Not again.

He swiped to answer, the screen lighting up with a face he had known all too well, one that haunted his every step even when he tried to forget it. It was Victor. His old mentor. Or perhaps his old puppet master.

"Damien," Victor said, his voice smooth, like a well-oiled machine. "We need to talk."

Damien's stomach churned. "What do you want?" he replied, his voice harder than he intended. He felt the weight of his own words like a cold weight in his chest. What do you want? The question seemed almost pointless. He already knew.

"I'm sure you know what this is about," Victor said, his voice laced with amusement, as though the situation were just a minor inconvenience. "You made a very bold move, Damien. A very stupid move."

Damien clenched his jaw, trying to hold onto his composure. He had expected this. In fact, he had been waiting for it. But hearing it come from Victor—so calm, so unbothered—made the weight of it all feel even heavier.

"Don't act like you're the only one who's been making moves," Damien snapped, his anger bubbling to the surface. "I'm done with Holt Industries. Done with all of it. I'm not coming back."

Victor's laugh was low, unsettling. It reverberated through the phone, filling the silence between them with its cold authority. "You think you can just walk away from everything you've built?" Victor's voice dropped, becoming sharp and threatening. "You think that's going to be the end of it?"

Damien's grip tightened around the phone, his knuckles white. "Yes," he said, his voice barely above a whisper. "I do."

For a long moment, there was silence on the other end of the line. Damien's breath hitched as he wondered if Victor would finally accept it, would finally leave him in peace. But he knew, deep down, that this wasn't how it worked. Not with Victor. Not with the kind of people who had been part of Damien's world.

Finally, Victor spoke again, his voice softer but no less dangerous. "You should know, Damien...you can't escape the past. It's not just about Holt Industries. It's about everything that you've left behind. The people you've wronged, the deals you've made, the alliances you've broken." There was a cold finality in his words. "You don't just get to walk away from that."

Damien's chest tightened. His mind flashed back to the world he had once inhabited—the cutthroat deals, the ruthless ambition, the never-ending climb to the top. He had made enemies along the way. People who were not easily forgotten, who didn't forgive or let go. And Victor knew this. He knew the damage Damien had caused, the reputation that had followed him like a shadow, long after he had left the throne.

"You think I don't know that?" Damien's voice cracked for a brief second before he regained his composure. "I know exactly what I'm walking away from."

Victor's voice grew cold again. "Then you understand the consequences, don't you?"

Damien's heart skipped a beat. He could feel the walls of his small apartment closing in on him. The weight of his past was suffocating him, suffusing the air with its poisonous presence. His life had been a game—one he had played without mercy, without thought for the people caught in the crossfire. But now, as the game came to a close, as the reckoning approached, the reality of it all began to sink in.

"You made your choice," Victor continued, the finality in his tone clear. "But understand this, Damien. There are some things you can't walk away from. Some people who don't just let you go. You've crossed too many lines."

Damien's mind raced, piecing together the fragments of Victor's words, trying to make sense of the warning. The realization hit him like a punch to the gut. They weren't just after him—they were coming after everything he had built.

"I won't let you ruin everything I've worked for," Damien said, his voice steady, resolute. "I won't let you pull me back into that world."

Victor's laugh echoed again, this time colder, more sinister. "It's not about what you want, Damien. It's about what's already been set in motion."

Damien's blood ran cold as he heard the subtle threat beneath Victor's words. It wasn't just about Holt Industries. It wasn't even about revenge. It was bigger than that. The game was much larger now, more dangerous, and Damien had no idea how far it would go.

"What do you mean?" Damien asked, his voice taut with tension.

Victor didn't answer immediately. There was a pause, a long stretch of silence. When he spoke again, his words were measured, deliberate. "You thought you could simply sever ties and walk away, but people don't forget, Damien. People don't forgive. There's a price to be paid for everything. And you're about to see exactly what that price is."

Damien's heart raced in his chest. He knew—he knew—that this wasn't just some idle threat. Victor had always been one to follow through, to make sure every loose end was tied up, no matter how messy or dangerous the process might be. And Damien had become that loose end. He had cut himself off from the machine, and now the machine would grind to a halt without him, dragging him back in, whether he liked it or not.

"I'm done with this," Damien said, his voice low, barely above a whisper. He was trying to convince himself as much as Victor.

But Victor's response was cold and dismissive. "You think you're the only one who can make decisions, Damien? The world you left behind has moved on. And it will keep moving with or without you."

Damien's thoughts spiraled. The decision was no longer his to make. He had stepped into something bigger than he could ever have anticipated. The reckoning wasn't a distant thing. It wasn't just a moment in time. It was the beginning of the end, and the consequences were already set in motion.

As he hung up the phone, the reality of it all hit him like a tidal wave. The past, with all its secrets and sins, had caught up to him. There was no escaping it now. There was only one thing left to do: fight.

Damien had crossed a line, and now he would have to face the consequences. He wasn't running anymore. The reckoning had come—and it would bring everything crashing down.

Twelve

Gesture

Damien sat in the dim light of his apartment, his eyes fixated on the phone in his hand. The screen still displayed Victor's name, the words haunting him in a way that he hadn't expected. Every ounce of his being told him to hang up, to ignore the message Victor had left earlier. But that didn't feel like the right choice anymore. The reckoning had come, and it was far more than just the whisper of a shadow from his past. It was an undeniable reality now—a reminder of the price of trying to walk away from a life that had claimed him for so long.

He placed the phone down on the table, the weight of it grounding him. His thoughts swirled, every possibility, every consequence floating around him like smoke, the edges still too elusive to catch. But one thing was certain: if he wanted to be free, truly free, he would need to do more than hide in the shadows. The past wasn't going to let him go without a fight.

The air in the apartment felt suffocating. The walls, which had once seemed comforting, now felt like a prison. He stood up abruptly, the floor creaking beneath him as he walked toward the window. The city lights outside blinked like distant stars, twinkling through the haze of the evening. This city was alive, brimming with possibilities, with stories still to be written. And yet, it was also a city full of unfinished business—a place where every decision could come back to haunt you.

It was then that Damien had an idea—a single, powerful thought that cut through the fog of confusion like a blade. A gesture. A statement. A move that would send a message.

His chest tightened with the weight of it, but there was no turning back. He had come this far, hadn't he? If he was ever going to truly break free, he had to show the world, and most importantly, himself, that he wasn't the man they had once known. That he wasn't the man Victor still believed he could control.

Damien's mind raced as he gathered his thoughts. The decision had been made. This wasn't just about escaping Holt Industries. This was about severing the last thread that connected him to that world—and it was going to take more than a simple farewell. It was going to require a move so bold, so undeniable, that there could be no coming back from it.

He dialed the number, his thumb hovering over the keys for a moment before he pressed the call button. The line rang once, twice, then the familiar voice of Elena filled his ear.

"Damien?" Her voice was warm, but there was an edge of concern beneath it. He could hear the unease in her tone—the same unease that had been in him for the past few days.

"I need to see you," he said, his voice coming out rougher than he had intended. There was no time for small talk. He had to move. He had to act.

"Elena... I need to tell you something," he continued, his words catching in his throat. "Something important. Will you meet me?"

There was a brief pause on the other end, a rustling of fabric as Elena shifted, possibly preparing for something she hadn't expected. Finally, she spoke, her voice calm but tinged with curiosity.

"Of course," she said softly. "Where?"

"The rooftop," Damien replied. It was the place they had shared many late nights, a place where the world seemed distant, where they could forget about everything else for a while. It felt fitting now—a space that was as much theirs as it was the city's, high above it all, yet vulnerable in its openness.

"Alright," Elena said. "I'll be there."

Damien ended the call and turned toward the door, his pulse racing. The next few minutes felt like an eternity as he quickly grabbed his coat and rushed out into the night. He needed to get to the building, to the rooftop, to the one place where he could let go of all the secrets that had been building inside him.

When Damien arrived at the building, he could already see Elena standing at the edge of the rooftop, silhouetted against the night sky. The wind tugged at her hair, and her figure looked small against the sprawling city below. She was waiting for him, her posture calm, but there was an uncertainty about her, something that Damien couldn't place but felt deeply.

"Elena," he said softly as he stepped closer, the sound of his voice carrying in the stillness of the night. She turned to him, her face softening at the sight of him, but Damien could see the questions in her eyes. She was waiting, trying to read him, trying to understand what had brought him here tonight.

"You've been distant," she said, her voice steady but with an undercurrent of worry. "I know something's been bothering you, Damien. I don't want to push, but…"

"I've been lying to you," Damien interrupted, the words coming out with a weight that surprised even him. There was no going back now. The truth was the only thing that could set him free, even if it meant everything else fell apart in the process.

Elena's expression shifted, her brow furrowing slightly. "Lying?" she asked, her voice filled with confusion. "About what?"

Damien took a deep breath, steadying himself. "About who I am. About my past. I've been hiding it from you—pretending to be someone I'm not."

Elena's eyes softened, but there was a flicker of disbelief in them. She stepped closer, her gaze searching his face. "What do you mean, Damien? Who are you really?"

Damien ran a hand through his hair, his mind a whirlwind. He wasn't ready for this moment, but he had no choice. It had to be now. The truth had to be laid bare.

"I'm not the man you think I am," he said, his voice breaking with the weight of the admission. "I was a part of a company—a corporation. A monster, really. Holt Industries. I built it. I ran it. I made deals, I manipulated people. I hurt people, Elena. And I thought I could walk away from it all. I thought I could change. But the past is…"

He trailed off, the words too heavy to finish. The silence between them stretched, taut and fragile. Elena remained still, her eyes never leaving his, as though trying to process everything he had just said.

"I never wanted this life. I never wanted to be the person I became. But I was trapped. And now I'm trying to make it right. Trying to make it better." His voice cracked slightly on the last word. "I thought if I ran away, if I started fresh, I could be someone else. Someone you could love."

Elena stood there, her expression unreadable. Damien couldn't tell if she was angry, disappointed, or afraid. All he knew was that he had laid his soul bare before her, and the future now seemed as uncertain as the skyline before him.

"What are you going to do now?" she asked, her voice low, but sharp with the force of her question.

Damien stepped forward, his heart racing. He knew there was no turning back. There was no way to undo what he had done, but there was a way forward. A way to make things right.

"I'm going to make it right. No more lies. No more games," he said, his voice steady now, with the conviction of someone who had finally made peace with his past. "I'm going to take Holt Industries down. All of it. I'll destroy it—rebuild from the ground up. And when it's done, when everything is burned away… I'll have nothing left to hide."

The words were heavy, final. The decision he had just made felt like the moment of truth. The big gesture.

Elena didn't say anything for a long time. She just stood there, watching him, the city's lights flickering behind her like a million possibilities.

Finally, she stepped toward him, her gaze softening. "Then let's do it," she said, her voice resolute.

And in that moment, Damien knew. This was it. There was no going back. His past was dead. And this time, for the first time, he would burn it all to the ground.

Thirteen

Rebuilding Trust

The wind whipped against the rooftop, the cool air brushing against Damien's face as he stared out over the city. It was an unfamiliar feeling—standing in the very place he had once thought of as his sanctuary, but now knowing that everything had changed. The skyline stretched out before him like a vast ocean, and the lights twinkled like distant stars, almost mocking him. His empire had once been built from these lights, from the very pulse of this city. Now, they felt like ghosts, haunting him with their cold, indifferent beauty.

He ran his hand through his hair, pushing the thoughts of his past away. He couldn't afford to get lost in them—not now. Tonight was about something different. Tonight was about her.

Damien's thoughts flickered to Elena. The woman who had

slowly become the anchor he never thought he needed. Their connection had been unexpected, almost fateful, but it was real, and it was something worth fighting for. He hadn't realized how deeply he had come to depend on her until the moment he had felt the pull of his past once again.

But how could he explain that to her? How could he tell her the truth? The whole truth? The secret he had carried with him, a dark weight he had buried beneath layers of lies and half-truths. The part of him that didn't belong in the life they were trying to build together.

A soft click behind him signaled the arrival of Elena. He turned to find her standing there, silhouetted against the lights of the city. Her figure was outlined in the moonlight, her features softened by the dim glow, but her eyes—her eyes were sharp, intent. She wasn't here for the beauty of the view. She was here for him.

"Damien," she said, her voice steady, though there was an undercurrent of concern. She approached slowly, as if she were unsure whether to close the distance between them or keep her distance.

He didn't move. He couldn't. He had no idea what to say. The weight of the moment felt suffocating. He had kept so much from her, hidden his true self behind a mask of indifference, always afraid that if she saw the real him, she would turn away. But now, as she stood before him, the gap between them felt like an abyss.

"I'm glad you came," he said, his voice rough, betraying the nerves he was trying so hard to mask. He took a deep breath, as if preparing himself for what was to come.

Elena tilted her head slightly, her eyes searching his face. She could sense something was different, something was off. The unease in her was palpable.

"Of course I came. I'm here, Damien. You asked me to meet you," she said, her tone light but tinged with curiosity. She stepped closer, stopping just a few feet away. "You said you needed to tell me something."

Damien swallowed hard, his throat dry. "I do," he said, his voice quieter now. He turned slightly, his gaze returning to the horizon as he searched for the right words. "I've been keeping something from you, Elena. Something important."

She froze, her body tensing as though she instinctively knew that this conversation wasn't going to be easy. He could see it in her eyes—the flicker of doubt, of worry. She had known something wasn't right. She had sensed it, but hadn't pushed. Now, she stood there, waiting for him to fill in the blanks.

"I'm not who you think I am," he said finally, his voice barely above a whisper.

Elena blinked, as though processing the weight of his words. Her lips parted, but she didn't speak right away. Instead, she just looked at him, waiting.

"What do you mean?" she asked softly, her tone gentle, though a trace of confusion crept into it.

Damien closed his eyes briefly, trying to steady himself. He had spent so many years building this persona, this mask, that he had forgotten what it meant to be vulnerable. To let someone see the real him—the person who was afraid, who was lost, who had made mistakes that he couldn't take back.

"I'm not just some guy who left everything behind to start over," he said, his words tumbling out in a rush, as if they couldn't be contained any longer. "I was the CEO of Holt Industries, Elena. The company you probably know about. I… I built it. I ran it. It was everything to me. Power, wealth, success. I lived for it."

He paused, his chest tightening as the truth spilled out, raw and jagged. Elena stood still, her face a mask of calm, though the storm brewing in her eyes was unmistakable.

"But there's more," he continued. "I didn't just run a company. I ran a world of manipulation, greed, and control. I made deals that ruined people. I made enemies who would stop at nothing to get what they wanted. I thought I could escape it. I thought I could just walk away and start over, but… the truth is, I can't." His voice faltered. "Not without consequences."

A heavy silence settled between them. Elena's gaze softened, but there was no pity in her eyes—just an intensity, a deepening understanding. She wasn't judging him. She wasn't running away. She was listening.

"You don't have to carry that anymore, Damien," she said quietly, stepping closer. "You don't have to carry all that weight on your shoulders."

He shook his head, his hands balled into fists at his sides. "But I do. I can't just erase what I've done. I can't change it. It's all still out there, and it's coming for me. It's coming for us."

Elena reached out, her hand gently resting on his arm. The warmth of her touch spread through him like a lifeline. It felt real. She felt real. In that moment, he realized how much he had been holding back—not just from her, but from himself.

"I'm not going anywhere," Elena said, her voice steady, her gaze unwavering. "I'm here. We'll figure this out. Together."

Damien's breath hitched. He wanted to believe her. More than anything, he wanted to believe that he could rebuild everything he had destroyed. He wanted to believe that he could be the man she saw in him, the man he had almost become.

But trust—real, raw trust—wasn't something he could build overnight. It wasn't something that could be fixed with a few reassuring words. It was going to take time. And it was going to take effort. Both of them, together.

"I don't deserve your trust," he murmured, his voice filled with guilt.

"You do," Elena said firmly, her hand tightening on his arm. "You're here, you're honest. That's what matters."

Damien turned to her then, his heart pounding in his chest. He wasn't sure what came next, or if he was ready for the consequences of his past to catch up with him. But as he looked at Elena, he realized something crucial: he didn't have to face it alone. For the first time in years, there was someone who cared enough to stand by him, even when the truth was ugly and the path ahead uncertain.

And in that moment, as the wind howled around them, he made a promise to himself—to her—that no matter what it took, he would fight for the future they could have. Together.

Fourteen

New Beginning

The city stretched out before them, the skyline a jagged silhouette against the deepening sky. The faint hum of traffic below mingled with the cool breeze that swept across the rooftop, but for the first time in what felt like forever, Damien didn't notice it. He stood there, next to Elena, both of them silent, waiting for the inevitable.

The weight of his words hung between them like a thick fog, choking the air and making it hard to breathe. Elena's presence beside him was a lifeline, but it also reminded him of the precarious edge he was now teetering on. He had done what he thought impossible—telling her the truth. The whole truth. He was no longer the man he had once been, but the very act of sharing that truth with her had opened a new chasm between them, one that he wasn't sure he could cross.

For what felt like an eternity, Elena said nothing. She didn't even move. He could feel her body close to his, but there was an invisible barrier now, one that separated them in ways words couldn't express. Every moment of silence stretched longer, heavier.

Damien wanted to speak again, to reassure her, to explain that he wasn't the same person anymore. But the words wouldn't come. How could he make her understand? How could he make her believe that the man standing beside her was the one who cared deeply, who had fallen for her in a way he never imagined possible?

Finally, Elena's voice broke the silence. "You… you're telling me you've been lying to me from the beginning?" Her words were soft but sharp, like the crack of a whip. She didn't sound angry, not yet. She sounded hurt—betrayed, even.

Damien's stomach churned. "Yes," he replied quietly, feeling the weight of his own admission like a physical blow. "I've been lying. I'm sorry, Elena. I didn't want to drag you into this. I didn't want to hurt you."

She took a step back, the space between them widening. The coldness of her distance hit him harder than he anticipated. "Why?" she asked, her voice barely above a whisper. "Why didn't you tell me the truth? All this time, you've been hiding who you really are. Who you were."

Damien turned toward her, his heart in his throat. "Because I thought if I told you the truth, you'd walk away. I thought… I thought I wasn't good enough for you, Elena. Not the man you think I am. Not after everything I've done."

Elena's expression softened, but her eyes still held a hint of confusion, as if she were struggling to understand the pieces of him that had never fully made sense. "But you are good enough," she said, her voice trembling slightly. "You... you don't get it, do you? You don't have to be perfect. You don't have to be someone else for me to love you. You just have to be you. I don't care about your past, Damien. I care about who you are now. The man I've gotten to know. The man I—" She faltered, her words catching in her throat.

The silence stretched again, but this time it wasn't suffocating. It wasn't cold. The air felt charged, like something was about to break free, something they both knew had been buried deep beneath the surface for too long.

Damien stepped forward, his heart pounding, his breath coming faster now. "Elena, I... I don't deserve you. I've made so many mistakes. I've hurt people. I've destroyed everything I've touched because I was too focused on power, on success. I pushed everyone away... until you. Until you showed me what it meant to live again. To feel again. And I..." He stopped, swallowing hard. "I don't know if I can be the person you want me to be. But I want to try. I need to try. For you."

Elena's eyes softened, her gaze no longer filled with confusion or anger, but something else—something Damien couldn't quite place. It was as if the walls she had built around herself were crumbling, piece by piece, as she took in his words.

She reached out, gently placing a hand on his arm. The touch was tentative at first, but it grounded him in a way nothing else could. "You don't have to try to be someone else for me," she whispered, her voice steady. "You just have to be honest. Be real with me."

Damien let out a breath he didn't know he'd been holding, and for the first time in what felt like forever, he felt something release within him. The burden of the past, of his lies, of the man he thought he had to be, began to loosen its grip on him. It wasn't going to be easy, not by any means. There would be days when the old habits would resurface, days when his past would try to pull him back into the darkness. But with Elena by his side, he felt like there might just be a way out.

"I don't know what the future holds," Damien said, his voice barely above a whisper. "But I know I want to face it with you. I don't want to be that man anymore. I want to be the man who deserves you. The man who can look you in the eye and tell you that I'll never lie to you again."

Elena's lips parted, and for a moment, he thought she might speak again, but instead, she stepped forward, closing the distance between them. The moment was electric, a shift in the air that felt like a promise. Her hand slid gently over his, her fingers curling around his, and in that simple gesture, Damien felt the first thread of something new, something real, something that might actually have a chance of lasting.

"I believe you," she said softly, her voice full of warmth. "I just… I need to know you're willing to fight for it. For us."

"I will," Damien said, his heart soaring in his chest. "I'll fight for us. Every single day."

The city lights flickered around them, but in that moment, they both felt like they were the only two people left in the world. No past. No lies. Just two souls standing on the edge of something new, something raw, something uncertain—but with hope, with a glimmer of possibility that maybe, just maybe, they could build something together from the ashes of everything that had come before.

As they stood there, hand in hand, looking out at the city below, Damien knew that the road ahead wouldn't be easy. It would be filled with challenges, with doubts, with moments of uncertainty. But for the first time in a long while, he wasn't afraid. He wasn't afraid of the future or of the ghosts of his past. With Elena by his side, he felt like they could face anything together.

And for the first time in a long while, Damien truly believed in the possibility of a new beginning.

www.ingramcontent.com/pod-product-compliance
Lightning Source LLC
LaVergne TN
LVHW010601070526
838199LV00063BA/5033